500 Affirmations For Wealth and Success Volume 2

Jos Brady

Copyright © 2020, Jos Brady. All rights reserved.

In the "500 Affirmations" series :

- 500 Affirmations for Wealth and Success Volume 1
- 500 Affirmations for Wealth and Success Volume 2
- 500 Affirmations for Love and Relationships Volume 1
- 500 Affirmations for Love and Relationships Volume 2

Introduction

To affirm is to declare a state of affairs as **already present** in one's life.

For example, declaring **"I am rich"** is an affirmation.

Similarly, declaring **"I never have a penny in my pocket"** is also an affirmation.

To your subconscious mind, both of these affirmations are equally true. However, the results you will get from them in your life will be very different.

Constantly repeating an affirmation, whether positive or negative, generates emotions and feelings and eventually crystallizes into a belief. This belief is like a seed planted in your subconscious mind that eventually attracts to your life what corresponds to it. If you want to harvest roses, will you plant thistles?

If you express yourself in a negative way, you will attract negative situations into your life. Fortunately, the opposite is also true. By focusing on the positive and affirming it, you will attract positive situations.

Unfortunately, most of us are "programmed" to speak and think negatively through the media, education, our parents' speeches and many other things.

Therefore, we repeat and believe these negative discourses and experience the results throughout our lives, unless we voluntarily change these discourses.

What are your ideas about money and success? What is your dominant discourse?

If you have a negative discourse, you will just repeat the same scenario over and over again and face the same difficulties.

In order to break this infernal circle, you must abandon this negative discourse and replace it with a positive discourse, both internal and external.

Affirmations are an excellent way to do this. Indeed, clear, short and precise affirmations are an excellent way to start controlling your thoughts and changing your life for the better.

It can be difficult at first to maintain positive thoughts and monitor your thoughts throughout the day. Don't worry. As the days go by, negative thoughts will become fewer and fewer and eventually disappear.

Be careful not to contradict what you say when you are alone, for example by talking with a friend.

How to use affirmations

The following affirmations are examples that you can use as they are. However, if you wish, you can modify them or write your own.

To do so, keep a few points in mind:

- Affirmations must be written in a positive way because the subconscious mind does not take negation into account. For example, don't say **"I don't have money problems anymore"** but **"I have all the money I need to do whatever I want"**.

- Affirmations must be written in the present tense. Rather than saying **"I will soon have 5,000 $ more in my account"**, say **"I have 5,000 $ more in my account now"**.

- Affirmations must be written as if they were already a reality. For example, if you want to move, don't say **"I want a new home that suits me"** because your subconscious mind takes you at your word and you will continue to want it for a long time! Instead, say **"I live in a beautiful house by the sea where I can blossom"**. By the way, if you have a clear vision of what you want, say it. **"I have more money"** is good but **"I earn 5000 $ per month"** is more precise.

- Say or write your affirmations in the first person, starting with "I" or "I am". You can also mention your first name: **"I, Martin, am happy to be a millionaire"**.

When you have chosen (or created) your affirmations, proceed as follows:

- As soon as you wake up and just before going to sleep, repeat them, if possible out loud, for a few minutes.
- Try to feel what you would feel if what you say was already realized.
- Follow your affirmations with a short visualization. For example, **imagine yourself in your luxurious new home**.
- Choose between 1 and 10 affirmations. You can change them from one session to the next.
- During the day, repeat them as often as possible.
- When a negative thought occurs, cancel it with a positive affirmation.
- You can write them down on a piece of paper that you will take with you and review regularly.
- You can write down your affirmations several times a day to reinforce them.

Remember that everything is energy and vibration. The more you nourish your affirmations, the more they become imbued in your subconscious and the faster you receive what you expect.

Repetition, faith and calm are the key. Repeat them dozens, hundreds of times and remain confident that the universe will respond in accordance with the request you have sent to it.

You are at the dawn of a new life. Do your part and the universe will surely do its part!

Note on affirmations

The following 500 affirmations have been designed to be useful to everyone. We are not all sensitive to the same things.

Some of the affirmations seem very similar, but their vibrational frequency is slightly different.

- Some are very short, others are longer.
- Some are based on reason, some are based more on feeling, and some are based on images.
- Some of them refer to the Universe, the Creator or God.
- The affirmations are written in either masculine or feminine, sometimes both. Feel free to adapt them.

Use the ones that speak to you the most and don't hesitate to change them whenever you like.

The important thing is to always keep the vibration of wealth and success in you. Be perseverant and the results will soon materialize.

500 Affirmations For Wealth And Success

1. My growing prosperity allows me to travel all over the world.
2. It is normal to spend money.
3. I breathe passion, determination and prosperity.
4. I am a lucky, happy, healthy and successful person.
5. I am a powerful magnet for money.
6. I feel incredibly rich.
7. I let go of all my inhibitions about money.
8. Abundance surrounds me. Today, I claim my share.
9. I own several successful businesses.
10. I bring money into my life on a daily basis.
11. I have a spirit of wealth and abundance.
12. The management of my business fills me with enthusiasm every day.
13. My bank account is growing every day.
14. I believe that everyone can be rich, including me.
15. My prosperity is boundless!
16. My life flows effortlessly and opportunities present themselves everywhere to me.
17. I can have and create anything I want.
18. New opportunities to increase my income come my way every day.
19. I have abundance in all areas of my life.

20. I am thankful to receive _____ € per month.
21. Money flows to me as easily as the air I breathe.
22. Money comes to me easily and effortlessly.
23. My finances reflect my ability to think positively about money.
24. My job is deeply satisfying.
25. My income is automatically increasing, more and more.
26. My employees help give my business the success it deserves.
27. Earning money is child's play for me.
28. Ideas come to me now that will allow me to develop my business and make it even more successful.
29. I attract money to me at all times.
30. I always find new ways to make big money.
31. I accept good things in my life.
32. I like to feel that I have money in abundance.
33. Abundance surrounds me and I am grateful for it.
34. I accept all the joy and prosperity that life has to offer.
35. A flood of money is coming at me right now.
36. I am rich and powerful.
37. My bank account keeps growing.
38. I'm opening my mind to greater prosperity.
39. I see prosperity everywhere.

40. I attract many lucrative circumstances into my life.
41. Prosperity in all its forms is attracted to me now!
42. Today, I am expanding my awareness of the abundance that surrounds me.
43. Money is as natural in my life as eating, drinking and sleeping.
44. Today, I attract wealth, abundance and well-being.
45. Every day, I make wise and profitable business decisions.
46. I possess a wealth of valuable skills and talents.
47. I run a successful business from the comfort of my home.
48. I am now realizing my plan for a life of abundance.
49. Every day, my belief in prosperity grows stronger.
50. There is an abundance of money available to me in this world.
51. I am open and receptive to all the good and abundance in the universe. Thank you, Father.
52. There is always an abundance of money flowing through my life.
53. I work enthusiastically to achieve my financial goals.
54. My grateful heart attracts abundance like a magnet.
55. My wallet and bank balance are overflowing with money.
56. I know there is enough prosperity for everyone.

57. My inner child accepts money.
58. I allow myself to be rich and successful.
59. I am attracting money now.
60. The more I contribute to the welfare of others, the more money I earn.
61. I always find simple ways to make more money.
62. I free myself from any resistance to money.
63. All the money I need is already ready to come to me.
64. I attract the perfect employees for my business.
65. I am comfortable with money.
66. My self-esteem and prosperity increase every day.
67. My positive attitude attracts large sums of money.
68. I respect my abilities and always work to my full potential.
69. Everything in my life is a choice. I choose to be rich.
70. I am financially free and satisfied.
71. All my bank accounts are filled to the brim.
72. I believe that money is a gift from heaven.
73. I'm in tune with the energy of unlimited prosperity.
74. My actions create constant prosperity.
75. I can get and I get more than I ever dreamed of.
76. I now draw from the abundance of the spheres my immediate and infinite supply. All doors are open!
77. I give myself permission to spend money for myself.
78. I can go into a store and buy anything I want.

79. Abundance and I are one.
80. I bring wealth into my life every moment.
81. Abundance is only limited by my unconscious.
82. I feel rich, I feel abundant, I feel alive.
83. I'm very good with money.
84. I am accumulating large amounts of money.
85. The passion I have for my work allows me to create real value.
86. Money is a spiritual entity.
87. Having money allows me to feel comfortable and serene.
88. I have the power to attract all the money I need.
89. My business is growing more and more.
90. I am very conscious of my abundance.
91. All the money I spend brings me contentment and peace of mind.
92. I can always get everything I need.
93. I see abundance all around me.
94. I feel rich and I am.
95. I deserve to have more money than I need.
96. I am grateful for the unlimited supply of goods in my life.
97. I have an abundance of wealth and I accept it now.
98. I travel to the most beautiful countries in the world.
99. I love life and accept my abundance unconditionally.

100. I choose to accept money in my life.
101. I have all the money I need for my personal needs.
102. Every day, in every way, I am more and more successful.
103. I allow myself to be imbued with financial abundance, and I generously share my wealth.
104. I create an avalanche of financial abundance in my life.
105. I create wealth easily and effortlessly.
106. The child inside me deserves to be rich.
107. I have more than enough money.
108. My thoughts are always focused on abundance and happiness.
109. I open my heart to receive the rich opportunities I deserve.
110. The whole universe is making me prosper now.
111. I send others thoughts of prosperity.
112. I see abundance everywhere and all the time.
113. I welcome my success with open arms.
114. I have unlimited abundance.
115. I deserve the unlimited abundance of the universe.
116. Money and love can be friends.
117. The universe provides me with an inexhaustible source of money.
118. I earn thousands of euros in passive income every night while I sleep.

119. I receive money and wealth from multiple sources.
120. I imagine abundance for myself and others and I get it.
121. I am destined to find prosperity in everything I do.
122. I am in tune with the energy of wealth and abundance.
123. I am a good money manager and I make sound financial decisions every day.
124. I like the idea of having abundance without any effort.
125. I have an inexhaustible supply of cash.
126. Life is fun, easy and full of abundance.
127. Money comes to me in expected and unexpected ways.
128. I know that perseverance is the key to success.
129. Great financial opportunities present themselves to me every day.
130. I am my own boss and I love my job.
131. I have excellent benefits in my job.
132. Everything I need to generate wealth is available to me right now.
133. I accept money from all positive sources.
134. I am able to freely express my ideas for making money.
135. I love the highest and best in people and I now attract the highest, best and most successful people to me.
136. The universe is safe, abundant and friendly.
137. Prosperity is attracted to me.

138. I deserve to see financial abundance flowing into my life now.
139. I have unlimited wealth and prosperity.
140. I am living a daydream.
141. There is an enormous amount of wealth in my life.
142. I am able to manage my enormous success with ease.
143. I have total confidence in my ability to succeed.
144. Money flows easily into my life.
145. Money and abundance flows towards me in a river of prosperity.
146. Money comes to me in expected and unexpected ways.
147. I always have more than enough money.
148. I respect my employer and he respects me.
149. I receive prosperity simply by thinking of luxury.
150. I am able to create assets that make me rich.
151. I feel love, joy and abundance.
152. I am an intelligent, successful and wise businessman/woman.
153. I earn more money than I ever dreamed of.
154. I am creating the successful business of my dreams.
155. I offer a product/service that people want and need.
156. Successful people are attracted to me.
157. I deserve the good life.
158. I am now attracting financial prosperity.

159. I know the world is prosperous.
160. I am rich beyond my wildest dreams.
161. I am prosperous, rich and happy beyond my wildest dreams.
162. I have a great entrepreneurial spirit.
163. I act every day for my financial success.
164. I allow the Universe to bless me with great abundance - now!
165. I have and always will have more than enough wealth and prosperity.
166. I have more than enough money to buy everything I need.
167. Every day I give thanks for all the wealth in my life.
168. I attract money as if by a miracle.
169. Prosperity is coming to me now.
170. Wealth comes to me easily and effortlessly, I am confident.
171. Prosperity in all its forms flows into my life.
172. My income is constantly increasing and I prosper wherever I turn!
173. I am now attracting the highest, best and most prosperous people to me.
174. I speak only of success and prosperity and my words elevate and inspire others.

175. I am more and more attracted to money, and vice versa.
176. Money comes to me easily and in all circumstances.
177. I already have everything I need.
178. I accept and embrace wealth in my life.
179. I claim my right to financial abundance.
180. Having money allows me to do more good in the world.
181. I lead a rich and abundant life.
182. I embrace money in my life.
183. The Universe constantly provides me with money.
184. Like a powerful magnet, I attract everything I desire.
185. I feel wonderful as a rich person.
186. I have total control over my financial abundance.
187. Money flows freely and abundantly in my life.
188. I easily accept to have an abundant life.
189. I possess wealth beyond my wildest dreams.
190. My wealth and success are inevitable.
191. My net worth keeps increasing, as does my bank account.
192. Abundance permeates every aspect of my life.
193. Attracting money into my life is fun and exciting.
194. I expect sumptuous abundance in my life and business.

195. I have more than enough money to provide for my family.
196. I allow abundance into my life.
197. I am the source of my abundance.
198. I enjoy my wealth and success.
199. My greatest good comes to me now.
200. My portfolio of wealth grows each month.
201. I always have more money coming in than going out.
202. Prosperity and abundance surround me.
203. I believe in myself and my business.
204. Money comes to me without any effort on my part.
205. Creative energy flows in all areas of my life and in abundance!
206. My constant spirit of abundance draws it into my life.
207. I am moving from thinking of poverty to thinking of prosperity and my finances reflect this change.
208. I am the best salesman in my company.
209. I let go of any resistance to prosperity, and it comes naturally to me.
210. Great wealth is coming to me now.
211. My income is steadily increasing and I give thanks for it.
212. Every day I am getting richer and richer…
213. Financial security always comes with me.
214. I love money. Money loves me.

215. I dream big, I expect a lot and I receive a lot.
216. I live my rich life with joy and serenity.
217. I have a golden life, I love well-being.
218. My positive thoughts about money come true.
219. Abundance is in me and all around me.
220. My annual income is _____.
221. I spend my money without fear.
222. Being rich gives me joy, happiness and peace of mind.
223. I am now on the royal road to success, happiness and abundance.
224. The more money I have, the more I enjoy giving.
225. I enjoy having wealth and abundance in my life.
226. My actions create constant wealth, prosperity and abundance.
227. I am prosperous and proud of it.
228. I am happy to have money.
229. I allow money into my life.
230. My business always makes a profit.
231. I am a wealthy entrepreneur who lives his life on his own terms.
232. Money is always flowing into my business.
233. My business makes money even while I sleep.
234. My relationship to money is magnetic and I attract it from all sides.
235. I love myself as a rich person.

236. Money is my servant.
237. I believe that more abundance comes to me now and forever.
238. I like to receive money every day.
239. I am a positive person and others like to do business with me.
240. I use my creative talents to create a successful business.
241. Wealth and money come to me easily and effortlessly.
242. Everything good comes to me easily and effortlessly.
243. I have confidence in my ever-increasing ability to create abundance.
244. All the money I spend and earn brings me joy.
245. Everything I can imagine for my business I can achieve.
246. I am open to all sources of income that the universe can offer me.
247. I create financial abundance by doing what I love.
248. My services are always in high demand and I make a lot of money from it.
249. Abundance is mine, now and forever.
250. Wealth flows into my life with a speed that surprises me.
251. I have the habits of a millionaire.
252. Prosperity in all its forms is attracted to me at a phenomenal speed!

253. I deserve to be a multimillionaire and I accept it now.
254. All my problems have now disappeared thanks to my wealth.
255. I'm at peace with having a lot of money.
256. I radiate wealth, abundance and prosperity.
257. I am grateful for all that I receive.
258. I focus on achieving wealth and success.
259. I have everything I need to do whatever I want.
260. I open myself to the flow of greater abundance in all areas of my life.
261. I look forward to a life filled with wealth.
262. I celebrate being rich.
263. My belief in abundance grows stronger every day.
264. I welcome and enthusiastically accept unlimited abundance.
265. Wealth is a positive expression of divine energy.
266. I feel deeply satisfied with my bank balance.
267. I am a magnet for prosperity and abundance.
268. I possess all the abilities I need to succeed.
269. Wealth pours into my life.
270. All my bills are paid in full each month and I have more than enough money left over.
271. I now live in a rich and loving world.
272. Success follows me wherever I go.
273. I can afford to buy the car of my dreams.

274. I am fully supported by the Universe to make money doing what I love to do.
275. I give generously and it is generously returned to me.
276. Prosperity is mine and I choose to live it.
277. I am very proud of my accomplishments.
278. I find it easy to set financial goals and achieve them.
279. My bank balance is growing every day and I always have enough money.
280. I run a very successful business.
281. I am a great giver and receiver of money.
282. I am a person who lives in abundance.
283. Every day is a day of prosperity and abundance.
284. My prosperity makes others prosper.
285. I breathe wealth and prosperity.
286. I set no limit to the amount of money I can earn.
287. I consider myself rich, and that's what I am.
288. I easily manage to attract success into my life.
289. There is prosperity in me and around me.
290. Money helps me to have a good life.
291. I am open to receive money and to succeed.
292. I attract talented, hard-working people to grow my business.
293. I am sensible with money and manage it wisely.
294. Today, I am more aware of the abundance around me.

295. Every day, in every way, my financial abundance increases.
296. Financial security brings me joy and happiness.
297. I have everything I need right now to accomplish everything I want.
298. I have a positive attitude about money.
299. I work with like-minded colleagues.
300. My company is designed for tremendous success and growth.
301. Abundance comes through me.
302. My life is full of wealth and luxury.
303. The whole universe conspires to make me richer and richer!
304. I am a money magnet.
305. The Universe is THE constant provider of money for me and I always have enough money to satisfy my needs.
306. I love to win money in the lottery.
307. I live in abundance and joy.
308. The more abundance I receive, the more I share with others.
309. I am thankful to be rich and successful.
310. I am always rewarded for the excellent work I do.
311. My finances are improving beyond my dreams.
312. I find it easy to attract money into my life.

313. I live in limitless lush abundance.
314. I have an abundance of creativity.
315. All I think about is wealth and abundance.
316. The more I am grateful, the more I find reasons to be grateful.
317. I feel inspired to make money every day.
318. A lot of money is coming to me today, and I deserve it.
319. My business attracts dozens of clients every day.
320. My mind is in harmony with the energies that create wealth and abundance.
321. My bank account is overflowing with money!
322. I manifest abundance through my unique gifts and talents.
323. I feel secure knowing that I can afford what I want.
324. I know that money is essential for a good life, but I don't have to make it my number one priority.
325. My business is growing stronger every day.
326. Every day, in every way, I'm becoming more and more prosperous.
327. Money is the root of joy and comfort in my life.
328. My prosperity contributes to the prosperity of others.
329. The more I live in abundance, the more abundance I receive.
330. I am a born entrepreneur.
331. I dissolve all false beliefs in me about wealth.

332. I have everything I need to be a successful businessman.
333. Money is an energy and it flows freely through me now.
334. Money flows towards me and welcomes it with joy.
335. Money is now coming to me from unexpected sources and I am grateful for it.
336. I contribute to the lives of others through the fantastic products I offer.
337. Money makes my life easier.
338. I easily, openly and freely accept abundance at all times!
339. Today, I open my doors to abundant prosperity.
340. Any resistance in me to receive more wealth is totally dissolved by divine grace.
341. I magnetically attract a lot of money in a harmonious way.
342. I think money is a wonderful idea.
343. My life is prosperous.
344. Attracting money is fun and I like the excitement it gives me.
345. I have a millionaire's spirit.
346. It's only natural that I have everything my heart desires.
347. I deserve abundance, no matter what.

348. I am a magnet that attracts all the good things in my life.
349. Riches of all kinds are attracted to me.
350. I am a powerful and constant money magnet.
351. All my dreams come true today.
352. I am prosperous in everything I do.
353. I am grateful for my ability to create abundant life for myself and my family.
354. I have everything I need to achieve all my goals.
355. My home-based business is growing stronger every day.
356. I am in a state of fulfillment, I have love and joy in abundance in my life and I am free to do whatever I want.
357. I am seizing every opportunity that comes my way.
358. Money always flows freely and without limits in my life.
359. I always have more money coming into my bank account than going out.
360. Thanks to my power of intention, I effortlessly attract all the wealth I desire and need.
361. I manage my business with confidence.
362. I always achieve outstanding results in my work.
363. My success is assured.

364. I deserve all the good in my life and that includes prosperity.
365. I release all my negative beliefs about money and invite wealth into my life.
366. I am an example of success and total success.
367. The child in me is rich and abundant.
368. The money I spend enriches the world and returns to me multiplied.
369. I am free of all debts.
370. I abandon all resistance to money.
371. I feel good with money because I know that I deserve it.
372. I use money to improve my life and the lives of others.
373. I am the rich heir of a loving universe.
374. There is always enough of everything I desire.
375. Money and I are friends and allies.
376. I easily attract into my life all the wealth I desire.
377. My financial possibilities are infinite.
378. Earning money is good for me and for everyone in my life.
379. Wealth floats around me all the time.
380. I can afford to shop in the most expensive places.
381. I am freeing every blockage that has so far prevented me from receiving prosperity.

382. I expect sumptuous abundance every day, in every way possible.
383. I am rich right now.
384. I am confident and successful.
385. Everything I need comes to me easily and effortlessly.
386. My life is full of riches.
387. It's so easy to open up to prosperity!
388. I deserve the abundance that is coming to me now.
389. I create money through joy, vitality and love of myself.
390. Financial miracles happen in my life every day.
391. My good is now flowing towards me in a river of success, happiness and abundance.
392. I always have everything I need. The Universe is taking good care of me.
393. I believe in my ability to succeed and prosper.
394. All my blocks to receiving money are now removed.
395. The money comes easily to me.
396. I am safe, all my needs are met.
397. If others can be rich, so can I.
398. I am grateful for my present and future success.
399. I manifest my wealth easily and quickly.
400. I believe there is enough money for everyone.
401. It is a wonderful feeling to know that I am financially free forever.
402. I am always where I need to be to attract money.

403. Wealth and success are natural outcomes for me.
404. I have the best job in the world.
405. I have the will to succeed.
406. I am comfortable with my feelings about money.
407. Only great opportunities are available to me.
408. Feeling joyful attracts abundance and I feel very joyful!
409. A constant flow of money comes to me from known and unknown sources!
410. Being a millionaire is fun and exciting.
411. Success and growth are the inevitable results of my work.
412. God is making me prosper now.
413. I respect money.
414. I am receiving money now.
415. Every day, in every way, my wealth increases.
416. Earning money is very simple for me.
417. I generate a large passive income.
418. I celebrate my success and I know I will be more successful every day.
419. My wallet is overflowing and my coffers are full.
420. Every day my financial prosperity is growing.
421. I release all negative energy on money.
422. I love to give and I love to receive.
423. My ability to make money is unlimited.
424. My mind continually draws money into my life.

425. I clearly see opportunities to earn money effortlessly.
426. Wealth is my middle name.
427. I trust that the universe always meets my needs.
428. I am able to make fantastic gains by working from home.
429. Prosperity flows to me at all times, in all ways.
430. I am deeply fulfilled by what I do.
431. I am destined to be prosperous and to share my wealth.
432. Reaching wealth is healthy and natural.
433. My bank balance is getting higher and higher.
434. Financial freedom gives me a sense of satisfaction and security.
435. I always have an unlimited supply of money.
436. Prosperity surrounds me, fills me and flows through me.
437. Compliments are gifts of prosperity and I accept them graciously!
438. There is an abundance of money flowing in my world.
439. I am at peace with wealth and abundance.
440. I am a euro magnet and prosperity is attracted to me.
441. Wealth is constantly flowing into my life.
442. I always achieve my financial goals.
443. I overcome obstacles and I know that abundance is mine.

444. Prosperity is mine now.
445. I believe I have the right to be rich.
446. I like being able to spend money on the things I love.
447. I receive money with joy - now!
448. I effortlessly attract everything I need to develop my business successfully.
449. I deserve to get rich and prosper.
450. Financial abundance is mine.
451. I have creativity and energy in abundance.
452. I am always lucky and I am very grateful.
453. I attract money wherever I go.
454. I welcome new sources of income.
455. I earn money easily.
456. I am the master of wealth in my world.
457. I focus every day on my financial goals.
458. I give myself permission to enjoy money.
459. Money comes to me from expected and unexpected sources, always in abundance.
460. Today is going to be a joyous and abundant day.
461. I am balanced and trust money.
462. My mind is a powerful magnet for profitable ideas.
463. My wealth is constantly increasing as I give more of myself.
464. I am a magnet for money, success, abundance and prosperity.

465. Money simply falls on me no matter what I do.
466. I am ready to fully accept money in my life.
467. I have a spirit of wealth.
468. I live in an abundant universe that constantly provides me with everything I need.
469. Money flows in abundance in my life!
470. I let the universe bless me in a surprising and joyful way.
471. I receive large amounts of money in my bank account every week.
472. Everything is going well in my financial world.
473. The world is good and there are no limits to what I can do.
474. I have a positive attitude towards wealth.
475. My grateful heart is a powerful magnet for all the good things in life.
476. I can afford to collect luxury cars.
477. I let go of any resistance to prosperity and it comes naturally to me.
478. My money is an energy waiting for my order to create good in my life.
479. I lead an abundant and happy life.
480. My wealth comes from the honesty I put into everything I do.
481. I can afford to buy all the luxury items I want.

482. My money makes me earn even more money.
483. I am a natural magnet for prosperity.
484. I choose to live an abundant life.
485. Money always flows freely in my life and there is always a surplus.
486. My life is full of success and abundance.
487. Money has a positive impact in my life.
488. I am happy to see that all my bills are paid now.
489. My home has all the luxuries I need.
490. I am in control of my success.
491. Money now comes to me in abundance in a perfect way.
492. Creativity expresses itself abundantly through me.
493. I am becoming a millionaire, every day a little more.
494. My life is full of everything I desire.
495. I believe in my ability to make a lot of money.
496. I am open and willing to receive wealth in all its forms.
497. Every day I enjoy more wealth.
498. I am able to show money when I need it.
499. I have access to all the money the universe offers me.
500. I attract dozens of customers every day.

www.ingramcontent.com/pod-product-compliance
Lightning Source LLC
Chambersburg PA
CBHW050306220526
45465CB00002B/852